KNOWING THE WILL OF GOD

by Gwen Weising

AGLOW WORKBOOK SERIES

Women's Aglow Fellowship, Int'l.
P.O. Box I
Lynnwood, WA 98046-1558
USA

ATTENTION

Aglow workbooks have been published for the edification of every Christian and may be used by any individual or group. However, unless a Bible study group is affiliated with Women's Aglow Fellowship, the name *Aglow* cannot be used in any way to designate the study group.

Unless otherwise noted, all Scripture quotations in this publication are from the Holy Bible, New International Version. Copyright © 1973, 1978, 1984, International Bible Society. Other versions are abbreviated as follows: TAB (The Amplified Bible), NASB (New American Standard Bible).

Cover design: D.A. Hitchcock
Interior calligraphy: D.A. Hitchcock

Printed in the United States of America
ISBN 0-930756-99-1

Write for free catalog.

Table of Contents

Introduction

Decisions! Decisions!

Everyone seems to be facing decisions: Should I pursue this career or that one? Should I marry or stay single? Should I minister here or there?

How does anyone ever find God's will for her life? Probably you've asked that question in one form or another many times.

Perhaps it will help you to know that you're not alone. Looking for guidance is one of the major pastimes of our day. Whether it's on a psychiatrist's couch, dabbling in the occult, or asking the advice of friends and counselors, people today are looking for guidance as at no other time in history.

There is only one true Source of guidance and that is the Lord Jesus Christ. All those who look elsewhere are doomed to failure, and little is gained except bad advice and confusion.

But even for those of us who acknowledge that God is the source of all true guidance, there can be problems of understanding that guidance. In this workbook we will be looking into the ways in which we can find God's guidance and also identifying the problems most frequently encountered in finding it.

You are not going to see, in the following pages, a road map of do's and don'ts for your life, but you are going to learn good, solid principles that you will be able to apply in finding God's will.

We urge you throughout this study to keep a notebook in which you can write down the specific areas of personal guidance you need. In each lesson you will be encouraged to apply the truths you have learned to your particular need for guidance.

By the time you complete this workbook, you should have a very good grasp of how to go about finding guidance for your life and for putting into practice the principles you will learn here.

1

Our Fears and God's Promise of Guidance

Getting Acquainted: If you are in a group, divide into units of two or three people and spend a few minutes telling your group of a specific time you felt God was guiding you.

Group Discussion: How do we know that God wants to guide us?

The Lesson

Our Fears and God's Promises

Most of us have many fears about guidance. These fears can be as varied as there are people studying this workbook. But as a rule, most fears fall into several definite categories. We're going to look at some of them and try to put our fears to rest.

Group Discussion: Share with your group some of your personal fears on the whole subject of guidance.

Fear #1. God doesn't care enough about me to personally guide me.

Personal Question: Do you feel or have you ever felt this way?

Although some of us might not express our fear in these specific words, our actions prove that this is what is in our hearts. This is a fear without foundation in the Bible. Scripture shows us a picture of a God who truly loves His creation.

Read Psalm 103:11-14.

1. What are the characteristics of God that are pointed out in these verses?

   a. ______________________________

   b. ______________________________

2. What action has He taken toward His children?

   ____

   ____

3. What does He know about us, His children?______________________________

Read Psalm 139:1-16.

4. Write down the specific things this psalm tells us about God that have meaning and reassurance for you personally.

Personal Question: Do these scriptures describe a God who doesn't care about us?

Fear #2. We won't understand what God is saying.

Most of us have had occasions in our lives when we have hesitated to go to God because we are afraid that we won't understand what He is telling us, and He will punish or reject us. This is another wrong idea. Because God does love us, His children, and has great compassion for us, He will always find another way to help us understand if we don't understand the first time. It's all right to question God, to say, "God, I don't understand; I want to, but I just don't. Please speak to me again in a way I can understand."

Fear #3. God is a hard taskmaster.

Many of us are afraid that God will ask us to do something we don't want to do or that is too hard for us to do. Here is another baseless fear.

Read Matthew 11:28-30.

5. What does Christ urge us to do in these verses?______________________________

   ____

   ____

   ____

   ____

The Bible assures us that Jesus is not a hard taskmaster. Jesus Himself tells us that His burden is light and His yoke is easy. His call to us is of the utmost tenderness and understanding. He knows we are weak and need His help.

More Fears

Fear #4. An imperfect past

Some of us fear that we have already done something in our past life to spoil the future. We have sinned in the past: a broken marriage, an abortion, a murder, or God called us but we didn't listen and went our own way—the list could be endless. We feel that these mistakes have ruined the future for us as far as doing something for God or as far as finding His will goes.

6. Read Joel 2:25 and write out the scripture.

7. What does God promise to do for His people? ____________________

Read Joel 2:12,13.

8. What are the conditions that will assure God's blessing upon His people? ____________________

____

____

Reread Joel 2:13.

9. Once again we see some very important characteristics God mentioned here? What are they?

____

____

____

Friends, be encouraged! God assures us that the wretchedness of our past is completely forgiven when we become children of God. It is true that sin leaves its mark, but Paul, who knew what he was talking about, encourages us to forget those things which are behind and move forward. God is in the business of restoration, and He will give back to us the wasted years. Not only that—He will make something beautiful out of our lives.

Fear #5. Secret sin

Many people fear that a secret or hidden sin will cause them to miss the will of God. Even David suffered from that fear.

Read Psalm 19:12,13.

10. What concern does David, the psalmist express here?____

____

It is true that sin may be a problem in our lives and, as we seek God's will, He will point out to us areas where there is sin. We may, even now, be doing something that displeases God, and the Holy Spirit may, this very day, put His finger on that thing and say, "I want to change this in your life."

If this happens as we are praying, we must simply and quickly surrender it to God. Before God will show us His future will, we must now be doing His known will.

Read Romans 8:1.

11. Those who are in Jesus Christ are free from what?____

If we are free from condemnation, then why are so many people almost obsessed with the idea that they have some unknown sin that is hindering them? It is because Satan uses this idea to discourage and defeat Christians. Rather than allowing him to do this to us, we need to take authority over Satan at this point, and in the name of Jesus, remind him that God is at work in our life and that He isn't finished yet.

Fear #6. Making mistakes

Last of all, many of us are afraid we may discover we are headed in the wrong direction. This can happen, but God knows that growing takes time, and as a loving Father, He allows His little children to make mistakes. He knows we need to learn about following Him.

When we come face to face with our fears, it becomes imperative that we confess them to God, asking Him to take them from us, reminding ourselves that He has promised to lead us, learning to trust Him, and then beginning to walk in that trust.

Now we want to take a look at the other side of the coin: What has God promised?

God's Promise to Guide

"I want more than anything to do God's will," the intense young woman said, "but how do I know what it is God wants me to do?"

How, indeed, does anyone know what God wants her to do in a given situation? That is every woman's problem. How, in fact, do we even know that God wants to guide us? We know because God has given us many promises concerning His guidance in Scripture.

Read the following scriptures and write out God's promises regarding guidance in each.

12. Psalm 25:8,9 ____

____

____

13. Psalm 73:23,24 ____

____

____

14. Deuteronomy 31:6 ____

____

15. John 16:13 ______________________________

____

____

Personal Question: If you have fretted and worried about whether or not God will guide you, what are some ways you can encourage yourself to believe that God will continue to lead you?

Read Malachi 3:6.

16. What do we learn about God in this verse?______________________________

Read James 1:17.

17. What words are used to describe the unchangeableness of God? ______________________________

____

Read Psalm 48:14.

18. What does God promise in this verse?______________________________

Read Matthew 28:20.

19. How long can we count on God's being around to guide us?______________________________

Read Psalm 121:3,4.

20. What comforting fact do we learn about God in these verses?______________________________

We can be sure that whatever God promises He does.

Read 1 Kings 8:56.

21. How do we see that fact borne out in this verse?______________________________

____

22. What part of His promise does He keep? ______________________________

____

God has promised to guide us. He will not fail, He will not fall asleep on the job. He will not leave us before the job is done.

Both the Old and New Testament give us a beautiful picture of the watching, care, and guidance of the Lord in the illustration of the Oriental shepherd with his sheep. God identifies Himself with a shepherd in the Old Testament, and in the New Testament Jesus calls Himself the "good shepherd." Let's take a look at what the Bible tells us about shepherds.

Read Isaiah 40:10,11.

23. Who is going to come like a shepherd?______________________________

24. What picture do you get of this shepherd?______________________________

____

____

____

The Bible abounds with God's promises to lead and guide us, regardless of our age or level of maturity. Our responsibility is to want to be led and to be obedient when God speaks to us.

Continue at Home

To search yourself

1. What fears do you have about finding God's will for your life?
2. Ask yourself, in the light of today's lesson, are your fears justified?

To do

1. Make a list of your fears concerning guidance, then apply the scripture promises of this lesson to them.
2. Answer the question: "Do I believe God has promised to guide me?" by writing the word, "yes" or "no" next to each item on the list.
3. Determine why you are unsure of God's guidance on the "no" items.
4. Pray specifically about these items.

To memorize

"For this God is our God forever and ever; he will be our guide even to the end" (Ps. 48:14).

Keeping Track

My fears about finding God's will are	The Scripture promise that answers my fear is

2

Our Need for Guidance

Getting Acquainted: Share some of the promises of God you remembered when you needed guidance during this week. If you are studying alone, list them on paper.

Group Discussion: Complete the following statement and then share what you have written with at least one other person.

I feel God is leading me when

Group Discussion: Share why you think you need guidance.

The Lesson

The world, in its foolish pride, denies that modern man has any need for God's guidance. But the truth is that none of us ever outgrows our need for His leading.

As a matter of fact, the need for guidance may be greater today than it has ever been in the history of the world. More decisions rest upon an individual's shoulders than ever before. Once parents decided what occupation young people would follow. Children either pursued the craft of their father or mother, or they were apprenticed to another suitable craft. A tailor's son usually grew up to be a tailor; a barrel-maker's son, a barrel-maker. Girls were trained in the ways of the home.

Another decision usually made for young people was whom they were to marry. This was usually decided when the couple was still quite young, and they had little, if anything, to say about it.

Today the choices for our lives, professions and marriage partners no longer rest in our parents' hands. Today, few women let their parents choose their future mates. We also choose our own life's work, our lifestyles, places of residence, etc. Within just the past few years even the choices of occupation for women have expanded tremendously. Now young women can consider a career in carpentry, fire-fighting, police work or heavy construction. Choices now pretty much belong to the individual. Christians have the additional choice of choosing to or not to move according to God's plan. When we are faced with important decisions, we must find some way to know God's will—His plan for our individual lives.

Personal Question: Write down a specific problem or area in your life for which you want God's guidance.

Why Do We Need God's Guidance?

Our reasons for needing the leading of our heavenly Father are too numerous to discuss fully here. Consequently, we will concentrate on three major reasons.

Read Genesis 1:26,27; 2:7, 20-22.

1. What familiar event is described in these scriptures?________________________

2. Who created us?____

Read Jeremiah 10:23.

3. What does this scripture tell us about man's life?________________________

The first reason why we need God's guidance lies in the essential fact that God created us.

Reread Psalm 139:1-4, 13-16.

4. Briefly summarize these verses.

Yes, God created us. He knows everything about us. In colloquial terms, He made the product and wrote the manufacturer's handbook. Therefore, He knows how we are put together and how we function best. He knows what we need to keep us in good working condition, and when we are "out of whack," how to put us back in good working order.

5. What else does the Jeremiah scripture tell us about ourselves?____________________

____

The history of the human race is for the most part the story of our struggle against following God's guidance.

Read Psalms 106:13-15.

6. What was Israel's fault?____________________________________

7. What was the result of their not waiting for God's guidance? ____________________

____

Seeking God's guidance goes against man's pride. Man as a whole is very proud of his natural wisdom. However, God doesn't see us as wise. He sees us in an entirely different light.

Read Psalm 100:3.

8. What does the psalmist call the people in this verse? ________________________

There are many references in the Old Testament referring to us as sheep. This same idea is contained in the New Testament as well.

Read Matthew 9:36.

9. Why did Jesus feel compassion for the people? ____________________________

____

Group Discussion: Why do you think God compares us to sheep?

The reasons why God compares us to sheep are not at all flattering to us. Shepherds tell us that sheep are incredibly stupid animals, most of which would not survive without the shepherd's loving care.

Let's look at some of the other implications given in Scripture.

10. What was the problem with the sheep in the last scripture read? ____________________

Read Matthew 10:6.

11. What was wrong with the sheep in this scripture? __________________________

Sheep without a shepherd are helpless, pathetic creatures. On the other hand, under the care of a good shepherd, they can mature and live safely.

Read John 10:1-18.

12. List the qualities of mature sheep that Jesus describes.________________________

____

____

Personal Questions: Does it bother you in any way to be considered a sheep? Do you think God's estimation of us is fair or unfair?

Group Discussion: Discuss some of the implications of Jesus' comparing us to sheep. Do you consider yourself a "good" sheep? What are some of the other voices that might try to lure a sheep away to disaster? Do you always *know* your Master's voice?

What is the prime characteristic or characteristics that makes us sheep-like in the eyes of the Lord?

Since the beginning of mankind, an intense struggle between man and God has been going on.

Read Genesis 3:1-6.

13. What did the serpent promise Eve would happen if she ate the forbidden fruit? ____________________

14. Why did Eve take the fruit? ____________________

Desirable for gaining wisdom! Natural man has always had a strong desire to be wise. And since the Fall, natural man has usually believed himself to be wise. God has another idea concerning man's wisdom.

Read Proverbs 12:15.

15. Complete the paraphrase of this verse: If we consider our own way right, we can be called ____________________

Read 1 Corinthians 1:25.

16. What does this verse tell us about both God's "foolishness" and His "weakness"? ____________________

Read 1 Corinthians 3:19,20.

17. What does God consider the wisdom of this world? ____________________

18. How does He describe the thoughts of the so-called wise? ____________________

Read 1 Corinthians 1:18-22.

19. What has God done with the wisdom of the world (v. 20)? ____________________

20. What is one way He has done this? ____________________

21. What did man's wisdom not show him? ____________________

22. What else does the world consider foolishness (v. 18)? ____________________

Reread 1 Corinthians 1:19.

23. What is God going to do to the world's wisdom? ______________________

____

The second essential reason why we need God's wisdom then is because God's wisdom and the world's (or our own wisdom) are diametrically opposed. In many cases, they are the opposite of each other, and the wisdom of each is foolishness to the other.

Let's look at one other essential reason why we need God's guidance.

Read 1 Corinthians 2:14.

24. How does the person without the Spirit look upon the things that come from God? __________

____

25. Why? ____

Whether we are ready to accept it or not, we live in a spiritual world ruled by spiritual principles. As a general rule, when it comes to the spiritual areas of our lives, our natural intelligence is virtually useless. Therefore, we need two things: first, we need to have the Holy Spirit, and second, we need God's guidance.

Read 2 Corinthians 10:3-5.

Paul is pointing out another important spiritual fact to His Corinthian converts. In essence, he reminds the Christians that we are engaged in a spiritual war with our enemy, Satan.

26. What kinds of weapons does Paul say he does *not* use? ______________________

Group Discussion: What kinds of weapons does the world use in fighting its wars?

27. What kind of power does Paul say his weapons have? ______________________

28. Describe that power. ____

____

____

____

____

____

Now that is real power! Man with all his wisdom has succeeded only in creating a world situation which threatens to blow up in front of our eyes. We live in a world that we have hopelessly polluted, many of those inhabitants will starve to death in the next five years. All of our medical progress stands powerless before new strains of disease that seem to develop daily; and not for lack of trying, we have never succeeded in capturing man's thoughts, short of making zombies out of them.

But the wisdom of God is available to every Christian if she will only accept the limitations of human wisdom, seeing it as the foolishness God does, and asking the Lord for His guidance as we try to live Christian lives and serve Him.

Continue at Home

To search yourself

1. What are some areas of my life in which I have been relying on human guidance rather than God's?
2. Am I willing to take these areas to the Lord and trust Him to lead me?

To do

1. Write out on the following page a list of personal decisions you are now in or in the next few years will be facing—job, marriage, new location, more schooling, decisions relating to aging parents, etc.
2. Begin praying for God's guidance in these areas.

To memorize

"Do not deceive yourselves. If any one of you thinks he is wise by the standards of this age, he should become a 'fool' so that he may become wise. For the wisdom of this world is foolishness in God's sight" (1 Cor. 3:18,19a).

Keeping Track

I need to find God's will for the following decisions of my life:

This week I must decide____

This month I must decide ____

Major decisions I must make that will affect the next five years of my life:

Major decisions I must make that will affect the rest of my life:

3

How God Has Led in the Past

Getting Acquainted: Share a time of decision-making in your life when human wisdom said one thing and God's wisdom said another.

Group Discussion: Complete the following statement: When Satan causes me to fear and to doubt God's leading in my life, I'm going to...

The Lesson

God's Leading in the Past

In any study aimed at learning more about God, one of the first aspects we need to look at is what has gone on before. To learn how God leads, we need to carefully study how God has led in the past.

It is interesting to find that not everyone in the Bible who received guidance from God was particularly looking for it. Yet God found a way to guide them. Let's see some of the ways God led them and what their response was.

Read Genesis 6:13-22.

1. How did God communicate with Noah? ____________________

2. How did Noah respond? ____________________

Group Discussion: Do we find any indication that Noah was surprised to hear God's voice? Share how you might have responded in a similar situation.

Read Exodus 3:1-12.

3. How did God communicate with Moses?__________

4. How did God get his attention?__________

5. How did Moses respond? __________

6. What further response did Moses have when God told him what He wanted him to do? __________

____

Group Discussion: Do you think you would have argued with God at a time like that?

Read 1 Samuel 16:1-13.

7. What happened here that would provide future guidance to David, especially in difficult times?

____

____

8. Do we read about any response from David at this moment? __________

9. What change came in David's life at that moment? __________

____

Read 1 Kings 19:9-18.

10. What are the two ways in which God spoke to Elijah?__________

____

11. What was Elijah's response?__________

12. What had Elijah been doing in the cave? __________

13. What very dramatic things did God use to get Elijah's attention? __________

____

Read Judges 13:1-24.

14. Summarize how God communicated first to Manoah's wife and then to Manoah. __________

____

____

15. Manoah's response is interesting. What is it? __________

16. What further presumption did the couple impose on the angel (v. 15)? __________

____

17. What happened to the angel? __________

Group Discussion: What do you think your response would have been if you had been Manoah or his wife? Would you have questioned the angel about God's will? Would you have detained the angel? Would you have been certain God had spoken to you?

The New Testament

Read Isaiah 6:1-13.

18. How did God communicate with Isaiah?________________

19. What was Isaiah's response? ________________

Read Luke 1:8-20.

20. What was Zechariah doing when God communicated with him? ________________

21. How did God communicate with him?________________

22. How did Zechariah respond? ________________

23. How did the angel respond to Zechariah's questioning? ________________

____

Group Discussion: Does it seem strange to you that the angel responded in such a way when so many other people in the Old Testament had questioned and nothing had happened to them? Why do you think it was different this time?

Read Acts 9:1-9.

24. What was Saul doing when God communicated with him? ________________

____

____

____

25. Was he looking for God's guidance? ________________

26. How did God communicate with Saul? ________________

____

27. You might say that God gave Saul the full treatment. How did Saul respond?________________

____

Read Acts 9:10-19.

28. Annanias was afraid of Saul, but part of Saul's response made a big difference to him. Although it is not stated, we can see from the events that it happened. What was it? ________________

____

Read Acts 8:26,27.

29. What guidance did the angel give Philip? ______________________________

____

30. What was Philip's answer? ______________________________

Two Sides to God's Leading

Read Acts 10:3-8.

31. How did God guide Cornelius? ______________________________

32. What was Cornelius's initial response? ______________________________

____

33. After the instructions had been given, how did Cornelius respond? ______________________________

____

In the meantime God was also finding a way to communicate His will to Peter in a rather dramatic way. Peter was a devout Jew, and part of the Jewish law forbade Jews to have anything to do with Gentiles. Peter needed specific guidance in this area.

Read Acts 10:9-23.

34. How did God guide Peter? ______________________________

35. What did Peter see? ______________________________

____

36. What did the voice command Peter to do? ______________________________

37. Although Peter was still in the trance, what was his response? ______________________________

38. What happened next? ______________________________

____

39. How many times did this happen? ______________________________

40. When Peter came out of the trance what was his response? ______________________________

41. Peter now received further guidance from God. This time it was different. How did God communicate His will to Peter? ______________________________

42. What did the Spirit tell Peter to do? ______________________________

43. What was Peter's response to the Lord's guidance to go to the home of a Gentile centurion? ___

____

Read Acts 16:9,10.

Paul had made his plans to go into Bithynia to preach the gospel. He stopped in Troas and there God gave Paul specific guidance.

44. How did God communicate with Paul this time? ______

45. What did Paul see? ______

______

46. What was Paul's response? ______

47. What was Paul's interpretation of the dream? ______

______

Read Acts 23:10,11.

Paul had been called before the Sanhedren in Jerusalem to explain why he was preaching Christ. After a rather trying day in which such great dissension developed that the commander ordered the troops to take Paul away so that he would not be torn to pieces by the crowd, Paul had an encounter with the Lord in the night.

48. In what way did God contact Paul to guide him? ______

49. What did God say to Paul? ______

______

Paul knew that from this moment on he was headed for the highest courts in the Roman capital city. God's will had been made very clear to him.

Group Discussion: As you look at all these people's lives, what can you say was the result of God's communicating with them in His own way? What do you think might have happened to you if you had been one of them? Think what might have happened if they had not followed the guidance God gave them. In a sentence or two, write out what we have learned by looking at these people's lives. What can be learned about God's guidance from these events?

God's Leading Today

Just as the Holy Spirit guided God's people in both the Old and New Testaments, He guides us today. We need to learn how to listen for His voice and then to obey His guidance.

Read John 14:16.

50. What did Jesus promise to send? ______

51. How long would this counselor be available? ______

The Greek word for Counselor used here is *Paraclete,* and it means "one called alongside to assist."

Read John 14:26,27.

52. What was the Counselor's duty? ______

______

53. What would be the result of this guidance? ______

Although the word *Paraclete* can be translated by several different words, *counselor* is very apt. When we are troubled by a legal matter, we seek counsel from a lawyer or a counselor, who advises (guides) us through the legal entanglements to a satisfactory conclusion. When we are in an emotional turmoil, which may be hindering our capacity to function normally, or when we have family or marriage problems, we seek guidance from a counselor, who can guide us through the maze in which we've become entangled.

Earthly guides may be able to help us somewhat, but they have only part of the answers. The Holy Spirit has them all.

But specifically, how does the Holy Spirit guide us today?

Read Ephesians 1:17,18.

54. What did Paul pray for the Ephesians?

a. ____

b. ____

If Paul prayed this for the Ephesians, shouldn't we, too, be praying for ourself and each other. There is a work of the Spirit which is supernatural, and that is the ability to discern right from wrong (often a factor in finding guidance), to have a Word of Knowledge or a Word of Wisdom which helps us know (by God's Spirit) what we cannot know naturally. It is a sudden insight, a "knowing that we know" without ever having been taught or told. These gifts are available to every Spirit-filled Christian for the asking.

Read Colossians 3:15.

55. What is to rule in our heart? ____________________________

Read 1 Corinthians 14:33.

56. What is God not? ____________________________

57. What is He? ____________________________

Group Discussion: Are you presently experiencing inner turmoil? Why? When we know we are in God's will, we can walk through some terrible experiences. Think of Jesus in the Garden and at the cross.

He struggled momentarily with the will of God, then surrendered to it. There is no further mention of a lack of peace. He went quietly to the cross in much the same way as a lamb goes to the slaughter.

When we think we have found guidance, if it is accompanied by inner peace, we may assume we are in God's will. However, if we experience turmoil, we would be wise to do further praying to learn whether or not what we think is God's guidance actually is.

It is possible for the Holy Spirit to speak directly to us.

Read Acts 8:29.

58. What did the Spirit say to Philip ____________________________

We do not know if this was an audible voice or an inward awareness. We only know that Philip acted upon the Spirit's guidance with excellent results.

Read Acts 11:27-30.

Occasionally, we receive guidance directly from the Spirit through a prophetic utterance.

59. Who prophesied and to whom? ____________________________

60. What was prophesied? ____________________________

61. The accuracy of a true prophecy is tested by whether or not it comes true. What clue is given

to the accuracy of this prophecy? ___

62. How did the disciples act on the verbal guidance they had been given? ___

___

A word of caution is needed here. There are many "prophets" among us today, some truly inspired of God and some responding to a zealous desire within themselves to be used of God. We must be very careful to discern between the two.

Read 1 John 4:1.

63. What are we not to believe? ___

64. Instead, what are we commanded to do? ___

65. Why are we to test the spirits? ___

We must not swallow whole every prophetic word that is uttered, no matter how wonderful it sounds. We are to consider the prophecy carefully in the light of Scripture. Then we are to pray about its validity, and, finally, if we believe it is valid, to ask the Holy Spirit to make it real in our hearts.

John gives us guidance for recognizing a false prophet. He encourages us to recognize the Spirit of truth resident within us.

In conclusion

By looking at the lives of all these people in the Bible, we can see that when God wanted to say something to His people, He always found the perfect way to communicate with them. For some the treatment was gentle, as when David was simply anointed with oil. For some it was dramatic, as when Saul was blinded.

For all of us, it is a matter of experience. God knows when we are ready to hear His voice. He has promised guidance, He has given us a multitude of examples of how He has guided in the past, He has provided instruction on the part the Holy Spirit plays in guidance. All we have to do, is to follow.

Continue at Home

To search yourself

1. Have you ever found yourself doubting the ways in which God leads you?
2. Can you take heart from the examples given in this lesson, that God is leading you?

To do

1. Look at your list prepared during the first lesson. Think about the Biblical examples you have studied today. Can you apply some of the principles from today's lesson to your list?
2. Pray and ask God to help you believe that, just as He has led in the past, He will lead you in the future.

To memorize

"But the counselor, the Holy Spirit, whom the Father will send in my name, will teach you all things and will remind you of everything I have said to you" (John 14:26).

4

God Guides through His Word

Getting Acquainted: Share an experience of a time when you tried to follow the leading of God, and others around you felt you were out of God's will. What were the conflicts you felt at that time?

Group Discussion: Tell about a time when you or someone you know was led to a particular decision through reading the Bible.

The Lesson

Guidance through the Word of God

People seek for guidance in many ways, but one of the most reliable ways is to search the Bible to see what God has to say about a situation. God wants us to know how He feels about our situation. He does not want to guide us in some magical way. Rather, He wants us to know Him so well that we grasp the desire of His heart.

That can only happen as we soak our minds, hearts and souls with His Word, the Bible. We need to be so filled with its principles and outlooks, and so sensitive to the leading of the Holy Spirit, that we know what it is God wants us to do.

The best guidance for our lives comes out of our daily walk and relationship with the Lord. Often it is our devotional time that God uses as an opportunity for giving us guidance.

Decisions concerning God's will should be made by a mind that has been reborn of the Holy Spirit and filled with the Word of God. This is not a secular mind at all, but a renewed mind. It is not a mind that is "conformed to the pattern of this world" but a mind that has been "transformed by the renewing" of the Holy Spirit (Rom. 12:2). It is out of the context of this *renewed mind* that we are able to test and approve what God's will is—His good, pleasing, perfect will.

Renewing is an ongoing daily process. Each day we must assimilate the Word of God in order to renew our minds. The person who has scripture in her heart has a special advantage. She has a "Bible think" that will influence her life.

Through reading the Bible we can find guidance by looking at examples of those who have previously been guided by God.

One person in the Bible who teaches us much about finding God's will is the Apostle Paul. Read the verses listed below and tell what Paul said about his next planned moves for God.

1. Romans 15:20-24 ____________________

____

2. Romans 15:28-32 ____________________
3. 1 Corinthians 16:5-9 ____________________

____

4. 2 Corinthians 2:12,13 ____________________

____

Group Discussion: Look at the key words in the verses above, the active words. Paul *planned,* he *desired,* he - *wished,* he *decided.* These are all thought processes. What does that tell you about one of the ways Paul went about finding God's will for his life?

Paul was a Spirit-led man, but he also used his renewed mind and his intellect to determine God's will. He made decisions and proceeded until God stopped him and headed him in a different direction.

Read Psalm 32:9.

5. What are we supposed to avoid being like? ____________________

____

6. Why? ____________________

Understanding is using our heads to determine the will of God—reading and studying the Bible, coming to understand what it says and means and learning how to apply its principles to our everyday lives. We cannot drift along like some horse or mule that is pulled by a set of reins; we must come to a place of understanding and knowing what it is God wants us to do.

Read Ephesians 5:15-17.

7. How is the Christian to live and walk according to this verse? ____________________

____

8. What is he supposed to do about the will of the Lord, according to this verse? ______________

We are not to squander our time, but to use it wisely to determine the will of God. God gave us a mind and God gave us time, and He wants us to use them both to walk in His will.

Knowing what is in the Bible, that God's Word is the source of our guidance, and that all other means and ways of finding guidance must be based on His Word, will help us to avoid trying to find guidance through unhealthy, emotionally unstable means. If we pray about guidance, if we take counsel from other Christians, or whatever means we use to aid us, all these must line up with the Word of God, or they are false guidance.

Some of our ways of trying to find God's guidance apart from the Word of God are not much different from those used by a young man I saw in a Buddhist temple in Hong Kong. In his hand were several clay pieces, something like broken clay pottery. After tossing these onto the cold stone floor, then, on his knees, he examined the way in which the pieces fell. He did this again and again with many prayers in between. His was a useless exercise, and our attempts to determine God's will apart from His Word are just as useless.

An Old Testament experience, which passed out of existence after the reign of David and about which we know very little, is the use of the Urim and Thummim to determine the will of God.

Read Leviticus 8:8.

9. The Urim and Thummim were put in what part of the priest's apparel? ______________

When the priest wanted to determine the will of God for the people of Israel, he put on the breastpiece with Urim and Thummim and went before the Lord. This practice was never employed for individuals, only for the nation as a whole.

Just what happened when the priest inquired of the Lord is lost in antiquity. Some commentators think that when a priest asked counsel of the Lord, the stones of the Urim and Thummim glowed more intensely than normal. This explanation may have been derived from the name, *Urim* which means "lights."

The only important facts to understand about the Urim and Thummim are that they were part of the priest's wardrobe, they were to be used only by him in inquiring on behalf of the nation, that the use of the Urim and Thummim has passed out of existence, and that nothing has been instituted to take their place.

Most means of divining the future have their roots in the occult and are forbidden by God.

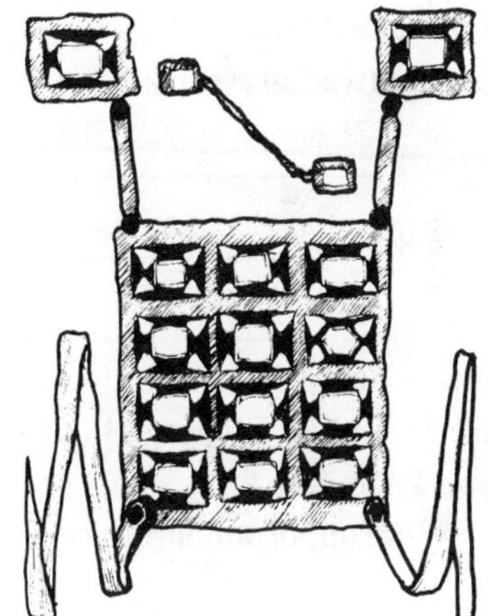

Breastplate of High Priest

Group Discussion: What are some ways people today attempt to discover the future?

Christians must stay far away from all those things which attempt to see into the future in an occultish way. Christians must renounce the use of Ouija boards, tarot cards, horoscopes and all other such devices.

Group Discussion: If the Bible is our major source of our guidance, then what should we do in regard to it?

We should certainly continually read the Bible, meditate upon it, and live it in our daily lives.

It needs to become absorbed into our everyday lives.

Read Psalm 1:1,2.

10. Who is the blessed or happy man? ________________________________

____

11. What is the source of this person's delight? ________________________________

12. What is he doing with the law of the Lord? ________________________________

Personal Question: How much time do you actually spend each day reading and meditating on the Word of God? Is that adequate for your life? Are you growing spiritually?

In many cases, out of the consistency of our daily devotional lives, we know exactly what it is God wants from us. This is God's Word at work with us, producing guidance and fruit. God's Word has become a part of us. It is important that reading the Bible become a daily habit. We cannot possibly meditate on what we do not have in our minds. We have to feed our minds so there is something in them about which to meditate.

Hard Decisions Require More Time

When we are facing particularly hard decisions, we may need to set aside *more time* to read the Bible. The harder the decision, the more time we need to meditate on God's Word.

Jesus set an example for us in knowing God's Word, applying it to avoid going against God's will. Satan did his best to get Jesus to go contrary to God's will.

Read Luke 4:1-13.

13. What verbal weapon did Jesus use to defeat Satan?

v. 4: ________________________________

v. 8: ________________________________

v. 12: ________________________________

Jesus knew the Word of God and how to use it to defeat Satan and to keep on doing God's will. Satan was offering Him the world and everything in it, but Jesus would not be led astray.

Read 2 Timothy 2:15.

14. What important instructions regarding God's Word are we given here? ________________

____

____

If we are going to the Bible looking for specific answers to specific questions, we are probably not going to find them in black and white, but something better is there: the principles by which we find answers and make decisions. Sometimes as we read, a decision we have already made is confirmed to us. Studying the Bible deepens our awareness of God, His nature and attributes, that which pleases or displeases Him. We come to know what decisions He would like for us to make.

Gerald Rowlands (in Aglow's minibook, *Alive in the Spirit,)* says about the written Word of God and guidance:

"The Bible is our most reliable guide and possibly the simplest one to use. The inner voice within our spirit is a somewhat subjective or unreliable experience. It may be influenced by our emotions or personal desires. Therefore, we need to submit such an experience to an objective or reliable judgment. The Bible is just such a source of judgment. It is not emotionally influenced or biased. It is not personally involved. Therefore, it is so much more reliable. However, we must approach it with an openness and honesty of heart because we can also make the Bible say what we wish it to say. There must be integrity of heart in our approach to it. Often people purposely look for a scripture to support what they want to believe. This is known as wresting or proof testing the Scriptures, and it is damaging to faith and sound judgment.

"When you sense a certain leading or impression within your spirit and you are certain that it is the voice of the the Lord, prayerfully submit that impression to God. Ask Him to please confirm it or deny it through His Word. Inevitably, once this has been done a verse or scripture will come to your attention that relates to the matter under consideration. It is really amazing how many different circumstances and subjects to which God can cause His Word to apply. Often in unusual ways, God freely gives His guidance through His written Word.

"God's Spirit will never disagree with His Word. The Holy Spirit would never tell you to do anything which is condemned by the Bible. He will never lead you contrary to the clear principles set forth in the Bible."

Unwillingness to Use Our Minds

Read Deuteronomy 32:28,29.

15. What was the fault of the nation talked about in this verse? ______________________

____

____

____

Group Discussion: What does it seem from these verses that God wanted these people to do? What was lacking in them?

Some of us, like these people, are unwilling to use our minds. We demand signs and inward impressions, rather than being willing to consider what God is saying through His Word.

Personal Questions: What means are you currently using to determine God's will for your life? Are you daily reading the Bible and letting it speak to your heart?

Perhaps the best way to deal with this unwillingness to use our minds in determining God's will is to admit we are lazy and undisciplined. Here are some ideas for dealing with our mental laziness:

1. Think ahead to what the consequences of a proposed course of action will be. Try to think all the way through, to project the possible outcome of an action.
2. Determine to heed advice, especially from those who care about you. In Proverbs 12:15 we read the fool's response to advice: His way is right in his own eyes.

3. Suspect your own feelings. Feelings are transient. We cannot depend on them as a reliable source for guidance.
4. Admit we are self-indulgent and would rather go our way than God's.
5. Admit we sometimes make decisions to escape unpleasant circumstances.
6. Admit we are capable of making decisions based on wrong motives.
7. Determine to wait for God to work things out in His own way and time.
8. Be aware that some well-known Christian, such as a person we see on Christian TV programs, could be influencing our ability to think clearly. We can be taking what he says as God's will for our lives without truly considering it carefully.

Group Activities: If you are in a group, use the choral reading at the end of the chapter. If you are studying alone, read it aloud. It is a prayer for guidance.

Continue at Home

To search yourself

This has not been an easy lesson, for many of us recognize our lack of consistency in reading the Bible, in meditating upon it, and in letting God guide us through it. We need to be "in the Word" daily.

1. Re-evaluate your personal devotional life. Do you see a renewed need for daily Bible study?
2. What do you plan to do about this need in your life?
3. What do you think the results regarding finding God's will in your everyday life, might be if you began to be consistent in reading the Bible?

To do

1. Make a plan or chart on the following page which calls you to account for daily Bible reading for the rest of this study course.
2. Write down any insights you receive through your Bible reading which relate to the areas in which you need guidance.

To memorize

"With all my heart I have sought Thee; do not let me wander from Thy commandments. Thy word I have treasured in my heart, that I may not sin against Thee" (Ps. 119:10-11 NAS).

Keeping Track

Today I read this Scripture portion	I spent this much time reading my Bible	God spoke this to me through His word concerning guidance

5

God Guides through Prayer

Getting Acquainted: Tell about a time when God led you to a particular decision as you prayed. Tell about a time when you prayed and felt no particular leading from God. How did you feel when that happened?

Group Discussion: God wants to guide us, He is willing to guide us, and He has promised to do so. Why then do we need to pray and ask Him to lead us?

The Lesson

Finding Guidance through Prayer

Read James 1:5,6.

1. What are we commanded to do in this verse? ______________________________

2. What will be the result of asking for wisdom? ______________________________

3. When asking for wisdom, what are the conditions? ______________________________

God has chosen to involve us, first of all in prayer and specifically in prayer for guidance. Although He could lead us without our prayer, for some reason, He wants us to be involved in the process, by asking Him to lead us.

Read Joshua 9:1-21.

This is the story of what can happen when God's people become too sure of themselves and fail to seek the Lord in their decision making.

Briefly summarize what happened with the Gibeonites and Joshua.

4. What mistake did Joshua make (v. 14)?

Group Discussion: Why do you suppose Joshua and the other leaders failed to ask God about this decision? Do similar circumstances in our lives also cause us to neglect asking God what His plan is for us?

5. What were the results of the decision Joshua made (v. 18,21)?

Joshua disobeyed God by not completely wiping out the inhabitants of the land, and Joshua had to allow the Gibeonites, inhabitants of the land, to live.

Read Joshua 10:1-7.

6. What happened later to Gibeon? ______________________________

7. Where did they turn for help? ______________________________

Because Joshua had become an ally of Gibeon, it was now his duty to defend them. The Gibeonites became millstones about the necks of the Children of Israel. (Centuries later Saul violated the agreement and massacred the Gibeonites. In retaliation, seven of Saul's sons were executed.) If Joshua had talked to God and sought His guidance first, this would never have happened. It pays to talk to God, *before* making decisions.

We often ask others to pray that God will guide us, we talk about finding God's will, we may even pray briefly once in a while, but how many of us spend even five minutes a day talking with God about what He wants us to do.

Group Discussion: If Christians everywhere began to spend five minutes each day asking God to lead them just for that day, what do you think might happen? If *you* concentrated on asking and listening to God's guidance for five minutes each day, what would happen in *your* life? What if we began each day by saying, "Good morning, Lord. I'm available. What do you want me to *be* today? What do you want me to *do?*"

Praying for guidance should be part of our regular devotional time. In prayer there is a growing awareness of the presence of God and a certainty about what He wishes us to do. As in reading the Bible, the best guidance comes as we daily give ourselves to prayer in our devotional time.

Personal Question: In the space below write down those things that you think should be included in your devotional prayer time. Don't forget to pray for guidance and for strength to follow that guidance.

A.

B.

C.

D.

E.

The time spent in prayer will bring about many benefits, one of which is gladness of heart.

Read Psalm 105:3-5.

8. The psalmist is asking that the hearts of those who ______________________________ will ______________________________

9. We are encouraged to do what two things? ______________________________ ______________________________

Sometimes in the Old Testament the word used for *seek* also meant to ask for an audience with a king, to desire to come into a royal presence. Those who enter into the presence of the Lord to seek His help and guidance will find gladness.

Re-examine Your Life Daily in Prayer

Another benefit of a daily prayer time is that we have opportunity to re-examine our lives for sin.

Read Psalm 139:4-7, 23,24.

10. According to these verses, what does the Lord know? ____________________

11. What was the psalmist's response to this knowledge? ____________________

____

12. If God knows all, even the sin that we commit, what then, should we pray with the psalmist? ____

____

____

____

It is not good to ask for guidance when we are harboring known sin in our lives. We already know the will of God in that case. To do away with the sin! Perhaps the harboring of sin is one of the main reasons we don't hear clearly from God in the area of guidance.

Personal Questions: Examine your own heart right now. Is there hidden sin in your heart that you know stands between you and God? Has it been difficult for you to find the will of God up to this time? Do you think the reason is your hidden sin?

If you realize that you have been hiding sin in your heart, take this time, right now to ask God's forgiveness for that sin. Surrender it to Him and see what He can do for you.

Read Matthew 26:36-44.

Jesus, the Holy Son of God, was also a man capable of failure. He was subjected to the same temptations and testings that we are, but He did not fail.

13. What did Jesus pray with regard to doing God's will? ____________________

____

14. How many times did Jesus ask for strength to do God's will? ______________

Jesus here admits His weakness. He saw what the cup held for Him—suffering, ridicule, death, pain and worst of all separation from the Father. No human would want to accept such a cup. But He overcame His reluctance through prayer, by asking for strength to do God's will.

We cannot face the hard times of life without the strengthening of the Lord. If Jesus had to ask for strength and willingness, then we must also.

15. What advice did Jesus give His disciples (v. 41)?____________________

16. Why were they to follow His advice? ____________________

17. Why are our spirits and body at war? ____________________

____

Personal Questions: What has your experience been with the weakness of the body and the willingness of the spirit? What do you do?

Read Matthew 6:9,10.

18. When Christ gave His disciples a pattern for their prayers, what did He instruct them to pray concerning the will of God? ______

Read 2 Corinthians 12:9.

19. What is made perfect in weakness? ______

It is all right to be brutally honest with God about our weaknesses in doing His will. God already knows our strengths and weaknesses, anyway. It is very helpful for us to be honest with ourselves, for as soon as we have admitted our weaknesses, then we can ask for God's strength. If we truly want God's will to be done on earth, then He will give us strength to do it.

Read Acts 13:1-3.

20. What was the church at Antioch doing? ______

21. What were the specific instructions the Holy Spirit gave them? ______

______

______

If there is a specific guidance problem needing a solution or answer, it may be well to set aside time to fast and pray about it.

Group Discussion: How long should we pray about a particular matter of guidance?

We should pray until we have achieved willingness to do God's will. Then it is time to quit praying and begin to act. Moving from prayer about what to do and beginning to act upon it is something like moving from the back of a knife to the edge. There's a risk you could get hurt out there; but that is where the action is. The harvest happens where the sharp edge of the blade meets the ripened grain. We do the will of God when we step out in faith and begin to act.

What about doubts? We may, even after we have fasted, prayed and sought the Lord for guidance, still encounter doubts. Probably everyone who has prayed for the Lord to lead still has some doubts about whether He is leading or if our own desires are getting in the way.

At some point we have to trust that we have the Lord's leading and proceed. Even if we are not sure we are going to be willing all the way, we have to trust that at *that* point God will take over and help us become willing. Trusting is risking—risking that we may make mistakes.

A young mother was finishing a dress for her child. The last thing to be done was to cut open the buttonholes. As the last buttonhole was cut the scissors slipped and ruined the front of the dress. Instead of despairing, she added a decorative trim which took care of the mistake and made the finished dress look better than ever.

In finding guidance, we probably will make mistakes, but God already knows what is going to happen. If in our hearts we are following Him as closely as we know how, He can work even our mistakes into His plan.

Praying the Psalms is one good way to ask for guidance. Listed below are several psalms which make excellent prayers for guidance.

22. Write out a prayer for guidance using one or a combination of several of the verses given here: Psalm 25:5,9; Psalm 27:11; Psalm 31:3; Psalm 73:24. ______________________

____

____

____

____

____

Through participation in prayer we begin to grow. It is by asking for guidance that we learn to hear God's voice guiding us.

Most of us are spiritually lazy. We coast until we are forced into a place where we must get down to business in prayer. God wants to guide us continually day after day, and that is best accomplished as we spend time listening to Him in our devotional time.

We need to quiet our hearts and make a place for God to dwell so that no matter where we are or what we do, we have an abiding sense of His presence within us. Momentary prayer brings momentary guidance. When we train ourselves to recognize God within us at all times, when we communicate with Him at all times and in all places, we will increase our ability to recognize Him everywhere and in everything.

Continue at Home

To search yourself

Are you keeping a regular devotional time each day? Do you, in the light of this and last week's lesson, see a new value in keeping a devotional time?

To do

1. Make a chart on the following page where you can keep track of your daily prayer time for a period of several weeks, or order an *Aglow Prayer Diary,* a tool to help you establish a daily prayer time.
2. Determine to spend at least five minutes of your devotional time praying about God's will for your life, both for the day and for the future.
3. Pray daily for willingness to do God's will.

To memorize

"I will instruct you and teach you in the way you should go; I will counsel you and watch over you" (Ps. 32:8).

Keeping Track

Today I prayed (record date)	I spent this much time in prayer	God revealed this about His will for my life

6

How Circumstances and Counsel Guide Us

Getting Acquainted: Break up into small groups. Tell about a time in your life when you set out to do something but circumstances completely changed what you did. (Some of these stories might be quite humorous now that they're in the past.)

Group Discussion: During the past two lessons we have talked about the importance of a regular devotional time as the best source for finding guidance from God. It was suggested that this week we keep track of our devotional time, and that we spend at least five minutes each day asking what God's will for that day was. Can you tell what happened when you followed this plan?

The Lesson

We Are Led in Part by Circumstances

In Port Antonio, Jamaica, the channel leading between a large island and the mainland is quite narrow. Large cruise ships come to the mouth of the channel and anchor there.

After a while a small powerboat leaves a dock on the mainland and speeds in the direction of the larger ship. Aboard the powerboat is a pilot who knows the safe passage into the harbor.

When the powerboat reaches the cruise ship, it pulls up to the side, and a ladder is lowered. Then the pilot goes aboard and the powerboat speeds away. After a short time the cruise ship begins to move slowly and carefully down the channel toward the dock.

Sometimes the cruise ship has a long wait before the pilot comes out. Sometimes it may even be necessary to wait for the tide to be just right. One wonders if the passengers aboard the cruise ship are pacing up and down the decks waiting for an opportunity to go ashore and see the lights.

It is vitally important, however, that the ship wait to enter the harbor until the circumstances are just right. To approach that harbor before they are ready or to rush the decision to proceed could mean disaster.

In finding God's guidance for our lives, we need to make sure that circumstances are lining up. This is one way of testing whether the guidance we think we are receiving is really from God.

Read Romans 12:1,2.

1. What does this verse tell us is the way to find the will of God? ______________________________

To prove, says Wuest*, means "to put to the test for the purpose of approving, and finding that the thing tested meets the specificiations laid down, to put one's approval upon it."

He goes on to explain that as a result of the Spirit's control of our mental processes, we are enabled to put our lives to the test for the purpose of approving them. Do our lives conform to the Word of God? Are we living in obedience to the Word of God? Does the Word of God saturate and control our lives?

If you think God is leading you through His Word, put it to the test. Try it out. As this is only a test, move with care. Be ready to withdraw if what you believe to be God's will is not truly His will. Likewise, be ready to proceed if it proves to be His will.

2. How is the will we are seeking to find described in verse 2? ______________________________

The "perfect" will of God means that "it is brought to its end, finished, wanting nothing necessary to completeness," Wuest tells us.

That pretty well describes what most of us would like to find when we know God's will for our lives. We would like it to be good and want nothing for completeness. And that is what God wants for us, too.

Wuest translates verse two: "And stop assuming an outward expression that does not come from within you and is not representative of what you are in your inner being but is patterned after this age; but change your outward expression to one that comes from within and is representative of your inner being, by the renewing of your mind, resulting in your putting to the test what is the will of God, the good and well-pleasing and complete will, and having found that it meets specifications, place your approval upon it."

When we have tested the will of God and count it to be good, then we can place our approval on it and get on with doing that will.

Group Discussion: God can and often does use circumstances to lead us. Think of a time in your life when God used circumstances to lead you. Were all of the circumstances pleasant? Were some of them uncomfortable? Does God most often lead you by planned or unpleasant circumstances, or by both?

Personal Questions: If you had a chance to get a new job—same hours, twice the pay, would you think God was using circumstances to lead you to a new job? How would you approach it?

**The New Testament, An Expanded Translation*, by Kenneth S. Wuest, WM. B. Eerdman's Pub. Co.

Even in something as appealing as twice the money for the same amount of work, we need to stop and consider if it is God's will. We need to re-evaluate our purpose for life and see if this new offer fits into these purposes.

First of all, with our renewed minds we must make intellectual decisions based on God's Word. In some cases, in order to make a wise decision we must also research additional information, other than that found in the Bible. Then we must wait to see if circumstances line up. If they do, we can then begin to think that God may be moving us in that direction.

Suppose a young man wants a certain girl to marry him—she has all the qualifications he wants in a wife. But if when he asks her to marry him she says "no," obviously, he has a problem with circumstances.

One of the considerations for using circumstances to guide us is to be aware of the part timing plays. It may be the "right job" or the "right person," but the timing is wrong. Waiting, too, can be the will of God. However, we do not always have to wait passively, we can wait actively. We can pray in tongues, we can be quiet and listen for God's voice. We can spend that waiting time getting to know God better and growing in Him. Waiting time may turn out to be some of the best time we have ever spent with God.

Read Psalm 27:11,14.

3. What is the psalmist requesting of the Lord? ______________________________

____

4. What instruction is given to the "waiter"? ______________________________

____

Read Psalm 37:1-11.

5. After you have read this passage, write in your own words the ways in which a believer is to wait and rest in the Lord. ______________________________

____

____

____

Notice that some of the ways we are to wait are active; do good, dwell in the land, delight ourselves in the Lord, etc. Some of the ways we wait are passive—being still before the Lord, being patient, not fretting.

Group Discussion: What problems do you see in using circumstances to guide you to God's will? How can we avoid those problems?

If we are trying to manipulate circumstances, we are headed for trouble: it is possible to read into existing circumstances anything we like. Or if we are stretching and pulling our circumstances to make them say what they don't, we will find ourselves in situations we can't handle and out of the will of God.

When God is in a thing, circumstances will usually flow together without our help. Our responsibility is to follow the Holy Spirit as He does His work.

Circumstances by themselves are not divine guidance. Write down some other things that should be considered as we are making a decision about God's leading.

Read Revelation 3:8.

6. What has God placed before us? ______________________________

7. If God is leading us in a certain direction and has opened a door, who can close it? ___________

____

Open doors (circumstances) are exciting, but what do we do when there is a door before us and we not only don't know if it's the right door, we don't even know if it's open?

Personal Questions: What would you do, in the natural, if you came to a door that you thought you should go through? How does that apply to what we should do spiritually?

We have to remember that a door doesn't come to us, we go to it and when we get there, we try the handle to see if it will open. If it will not, we might lean on it a little. We might even bang or kick it to see if it's stuck.

Finding God's will through circumstances becomes a little more complicated when two or more very good choices are available. We are faced with two excellent positions; equal pay, equal benefits, both in pleasant surroundings. Sometimes we are tempted to ask, "God, why are You doing this to me?"

Group Discussion: What might God's reasons be for giving us two opportunities at the same time?

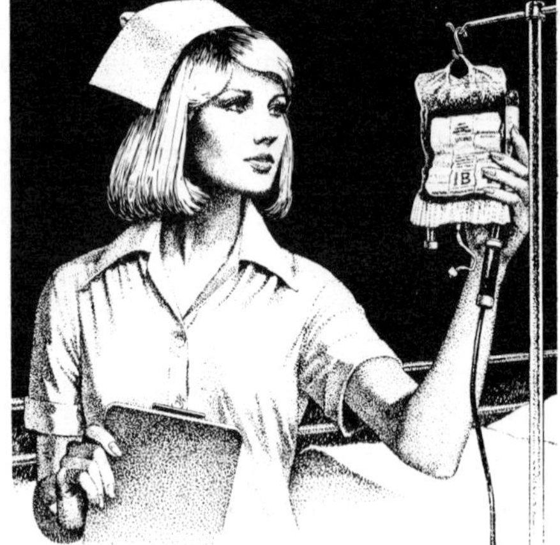

When we choose the general direction of our lives (our vocation), God then leads us through the responsibilities of that vocation. If God has led you into the field of nursing, then He expects you to report to work on time, wear a clean uniform, be ready to put in an honest day's work in the most careful professional way possible. It is your responsibility! As you fulfill that responsibility, He will show you the next move He wants you to make.

Some other circumstances God uses are the bringing of certain people or events into our lives to guide us, a book that gives insight, or the timing of an event.

One last thing to consider about the way in which God uses circumstances to guide us is the state of our comfort. Some of us are very comfortable right where we are and would never move if we didn't have to. In order to get us moving in another direction, God sometimes allows our circumstances to become very uncomfortable.

A student once asked, "How uncomfortable do you have to get before you are ready to move?" The answer is that God will make it just as uncomfortable as necessary to get us moving.

The counsel of other Christians helps us find God's will.

A popular song says, "People who need people are the luckiest people in the world." Christians are not lucky, we're blessed, and we are people who need people. One of the great tragedies of the Church is that in practice we give so little thought to relating to one another—to helping guide one another, to caring what happens to each other.

Group Discussion: When we talk about Christian fellowship, what is the first picture that comes to your mind? Is this truly Christian fellowship?

The truth is that when we come together we are reluctant to share ourselves with others. We live behind masks, not wanting to share our inner selves with others, to reveal what we truly are. But all through the New Testament, Christianity and fellowship are closely linked.

Read 2 Thessalonians 1:3 in the American Standard Bible.

8. Who is being addressed in this verse? ______________________

9. When the faith of the brethren is greatly enlarged, what should the result be? ______________________

Read Colossians 1:3,4.

10. What does Paul commend the Colossian Christians for? ______________________

Read 2 Corinthians 8:7,8.

11. What did the Corinthian Church excel in according to these verses? ______________________

12. What added admonition did Paul give in encouraging them to continue? ______________________

Read Philemon 4:5.

13. Why did Paul give thanks for Philemon? ______________________

Read Acts 2:41-47.

14. What is the connection here between faith and love for the saints? ______________________

Group Discussion: Think about the verses you have just read. What common idea is expressed in all of them? What does that mean to us today?

We need each other. We need the advice and counsel we receive from Christian brothers and sisters who care deeply about us. Doesn't it make sense that if Christianity and fellowship are so closely linked, then we should not be making decisions about God's will apart from our relationship and counsel with other Christians.

Read Proverbs 11:14.

15. What is the result of not seeking guidance? ______________________

16. Where do we find victory in this matter? ______________________

Read Proverbs 12:15.

17. How do we determine who is the fool and who is the wise man according to this verse? ______________________

When we are facing major decisions, we would do well to seek counsel of godly, mature Christians who truly care about what happens to us.

One of the benefits of counsel is that talking with another person helps us think creatively about our decision. We hear our own voice telling the other person our questions and the problems we face. This helps us clarify our thinking.

When we counsel with several people and most of them agree as to a certain course of action or feel we are suited for a certain profession, etc., we need to give consideration to what they are saying. There's safety in many advisors.

On the other hand, although we need to seriously consider their views, the final decision rests with us. Our advisors may not all agree, but their varied views cause us to consider all sides of the issue, to be well-rounded in our consideration of the decision to be made.

Bear in mind that counsel by the most wonderful, well-meaning Christian friends is still not divine guidance. We need *also* to seek the face of God and see if He agrees with our counselors.

We cannot lean on others to make our decisions for us. A young Christian woman came to her pastor for counsel. She wanted his approval to marry an unbeliever. Of course, she knew that the Bible said about the matter and she probably knew what the pastor would say. However, what she really wanted, was someone else to assume responsibility. In the event that something went wrong, she would then be able to say, "But you said..." This wise pastor would not even give her an answer because she already knew what God's will was.

Some ideas about where to seek counsel:

1. Seek advice from a variety of people. Include in this some who might not agree with you.
2. Seek advice from believers (See Ps. 1:1).
3. Seek advice from those who know you well. Parents, close friends, family, pastors and other spiritual leaders who care deeply about you.
4. Recognize that there may be times in your life when you will need long-term counseling from professionals—psychologists or psychiatrists. It is important to go to a Christian, however, if at all possible. Non-Christians operate and think from a different set of values and can do great damage to a believer's faith in a counseling setting.

We must realize that counseling eventually comes to an end, and we then have to act on the advice we have been given. We need, also, to remember that just as circumstances by themselves are not a good basis for making decisions on guidance, neither is counsel by itself. We need to base our decisions on the Word of God, on prayer, on circumstances, and on counsel.

As in any new skill, it takes practice to know what God is saying and how He is leading. God is not in a hurry. He wants you to grow through each new experience of your life, to become more like His Son, Jesus Christ. So give Him plenty of time to work in your life.

Continue at Home

To search yourself

1. Spend some time thinking about times when you have counseled with another about a decision. Was the advice wise and good? Why or why not? If today you were facing a decision, where would you turn for counsel?

2. Read James 3:13-15. How do you think these verses relate to the whole subject of counsel? What two kinds of wisdom are depicted here? Which kind of wisdom would you like to find in the person with whom you are counseling? Could you possibly become a person who has the wisdom that will help other people? How can that happen?

To do

1. In your notebook write down the names, addresses and telephone numbers of three or four people you could turn to when making an important decision.
2. The next time you have an important decision to make, write down all the ways circumstances seem to be working against your decision, on the left hand side of the page. On the right, write down all the ways circumstances seem to be working for your decision.

To memorize

"Blessed is the man who does not walk in the counsel of the wicked or stand in the way of sinners or sit in the seat of mockers. But his delight is in the law of the Lord, and on his law he meditates day and night" (Ps. 1:1,2).

Keeping Track

Decision to be made: ____________________

Circumstances which say go ahead	Circumstances which tell me to wait	Circumstances which tell me this is not best for me at this time

7

Supernatural and Inward Leadings

Getting Acquainted: Have you received counsel in the community of Christians this week? As a natural part of being together with other Christians, have you been encouraged, uplifted, admonished or even been given direct guidance?

Have you seen how God has used circumstances to lead you? Share with the others in the group.

Group Discussion: What are some kinds of supernatural guidance you think we might expect?

The Lesson

Receiving Supernatural Guidance

When people talk about receiving supernatural guidance, they are usually talking about two kinds:

1. Direct guidance—a vision, a sign, a voice—something which comes directly to the individual.
2. Indirect guidance—A prophetic word, either public or private, which the Spirit quickens to your heart as being for you.

Supernatural guidance is real and valid, and for the Spirit-filled believer, an important source of guidance; but many are confused about this whole area. We must always remember that no matter what the supernatural guidance—a vision, a prophecy, a sign—we still have to use our minds to understand what it is God is trying to say to us through the supernatural act.

It is also possible for us to misinterpret our own personal desires as being the supernatural voice of God. It is possible to hear voices other than God's. Sometimes what we are hearing is no more than our over-strict conscience telling us it is God's will that we try harder.

1. When the boy Samuel first heard God's voice, whom did he think was calling him? ___________

2. How many times did Samuel mistakenly think Eli was calling? ___________

3. Why did he mistake the Lord's voice for Eli's? ___________

____

Read John 10:4,5.

4. To whom do the sheep respond? ___________

5. What voice will they not follow? ___________

Shepherds in Bible times led their sheep to common watering holes. Often several bands of sheep mixed together there. When the time came to move on and separate the sheep, the shepherd would give a certain call which his own sheep knew. As he began to walk on, his sheep would leave the milling throng to follow him. They could hear the other shepherds' calls, but they would not follow a stranger's voice.

Group Discussion: What important element necessary for guidance is indicated in the two scriptures discussed above?

It is vitally important that we know God's voice and that we daily listen for it. That is the only way we can come to hear Him above the noises of the milling throng of our world.

A woman badly needed a job shortly after she had been saved. One morning while she was lying in bed, she began to pray about it. "God, what shall I do about a job?" she asked.

Back came an audible voice which told her, "Go to Aglow."

"What's Aglow?" she answered back, honestly not knowing about the organization. She had to search for Aglow, and when she found it there were two positions open. She was soon hired for one of them.

God knew that this young woman, new to the Christian way of life, needed something to get her going in His direction, and so He gave her audible, direct, supernatural guidance.

Read 1 John 2:27.

6. What do believers have to enable them? ___________

____

____

7. What function does this anointing have in our lives? ___________

____

____

8. The Spirit teaches us—leads each of us. Look at the scripture below to see some of the ways He led individuals in the early church. After you have looked up and written out the answers, circle the words which give direction.

Acts 8:29 ___________

Acts 10:19 ___________

Acts 13:2 ______________________________

Acts 15:28 ______________________________

Acts 16:6 ______________________________

Supernatural guidance often comes while we are being led to do something we would not otherwise consider doing, such as the young woman in the story above, either because of ignorance or because it is so different from anything we've done so far. It is a strong push in a new direction you might not have considered before. However, we cannot sit waiting for that kind of special guidance. We often have to walk by faith, relying on God'sWord, prayer, counsel and circumstances to guide us. If we are strong, God is free to intervene at any time with a supernatural act to stop us, turn us around and send us off in an entirely different direction.

Personal Prophecy and Guidance

The times when personal prophecy was God's means of talking to individuals in the New Testament are rather limited. Even in the life of the Apostle Paul, these supernatural acts of guidance (personal prophecy) are separated by months and years of walking solely by faith.

Read Acts 13:1,2.

9. What did the Holy Spirit do with regard to Paul and Barnabas? ______________________________

Group Discussion: How does the Holy Spirit operate within the Body of Christ? What vehicle does He use?

Personal Question: Imagine what happened in the church in Antioch at the time Paul and Barnabas were "set apart" and write a description in your own words below.

Read Acts 21:10-14.

10. What was Agabus' prophecy concerning Paul? ______________________________

11. By what authority did Agabus say he was speaking? ______

12. What was the reaction of the other Christians? ______

13. What was Paul's response? ______

14. How does Paul conclude his remarks to them? ______

______

______

As always Paul was, first of all, more interested in doing God's will than in being safe or comfortable. He heard and understood the personal prophecy, but in his heart he was convinced it was for information only and not for direction. He proceeded with his plans and went to Jerusalem.

Read Acts 21:27-30.

15. What immediately happened? ______

Paul's choice to go to Jerusalem began a series of events which eventually led to his martyrdom.

Personal Questions: How do you think you might have responded to these circumstances if you had been Paul? If you have ever had a personal prophecy given to you, what was your response?

Read 2 Timothy 1:6.

16. Paul here encourages Timothy to action, to kindle afresh the gift of God, which came to him

in what way? ______

It would seem that Timothy had been given a personal prophecy by Paul for that particular ministry to which God was calling him. We are not given any more information as to what the gift was or the prophecy said.

Those are the main incidents of personal prophecy given in the New Testament. It seems to be the exception rather than the rule that God speaks to individuals through personal prophecy. When it does happen, it can be put to a test.

Read 1 Corinthians 14:3.

17. What are the three guidelines for prophecy:

a. ______

b. ______

c. ______

It is the Holy Spirit's function to build up believers, to comfort them, to inspire them to action. Any personal prophecy which produces fear, tears down trust or confidence, or discourages the believer should be carefully evaluated.

Usually personal prophecy will be a verification of something God has already been dealing with us about. We, too, as Spirit-filled believers have direct access to God. In most cases His Holy Spirit can deal directly with us and He needs no other intermediary.

One story of a personal prophecy given for consolation happened a few years ago in California. A man was being sent to Vietnam as a pilot to fly small planes which led the larger planes in for bombing runs. These planes flew very low and were often shot down. It was dangerous work and many pilots never returned from these missions.

His wife, left behind with four small children, was terrified that she would never see him again. On the night of his departure, they were in church together and during that service the Holy Spirit spoke a word of comfort to their distraught hearts through another individual in the church. It was a message that the husband would return unscathed.

If a personal prophecy is truly from the Holy Spirit, it will be fulfilled just as it was spoken. This man, in spite of involvement in a plane crash, returned from Vietnam without a scratch. The Holy Spirit truly had spoken.

Some individuals have told how, through personal prophecy, they have been given confidence to pursue a certain course for their life about which God had been dealing with them at the time. Fear of failure had kept them from setting out to do God's will. The personal prophecy given to them served as an exhortation to go ahead and do what God was already dealing with them about.

Finding Guidance through Signs

A man named Gideon started a practice known as "putting out a fleece" or "fleecing," which continues to this day.

Read Judges 6:36-40.

18. Read the passage and write out a description of what Gideon did. ______________________

____

____

This is the *only place* in the Bible where such a practice took place and yet, today, there are Christians who ask for signs, which are as unrelated to the issue as a fleece is to a war, to determine the will of God.

Read Proverbs 16:33.

19. What practice in determining guidance do we see here? ______________________

This practice came from ancient times when bits, or small tablets of wood or stone, sometimes inscribed with the names of people, were put into a garment (or a lap), from which they were cast after being shaken together. The first lot which fell out was the chosen one.

Fleecing was never used again in the Bible, and the casting of lots is not mentioned after the day of Pentecost. We find no record of their ever being used again to determine guidance. Today God's Holy Spirit who knows the perfect will of God lives within us. He will show us God's will.

Fleecing remains a temptation to some Christians. We want to know where God is leading, and we are often afraid to just trust Him. We try, by seeking a sign, to see where He is leading. Fleecing is a mark of spiritual immaturity, of abandoning our personal responsibility. God wants us to grow toward spiritual maturity, trust and responsibility.

This is not to say that we can never ask for a sign that God is leading us in a certain direction. Fleecing is a sign that is totally unrelated to an issue. For example, when a friend was trying to decide whether or not she should buy a certain house, she did not pray, "God let a black cat fall out of a tree and land on my feet right now if this is Your will." That would have been a request totally unrelated to the purchase of a house.

However, she did pray, "God, if this is the house You want me to have, let the owners take $1,000.00 less than they are asking. You know, Lord, the realtor thinks the house is over-priced, and we really can't afford to pay more than the house is worth. We need to know Your will in this matter, so please help us."

This was a request related to the issue and God honored it. The owner dropped the price of the house $1,000.00, and in a few weeks the friend and her family moved into it. It has been the perfect home for their needs.

Inward Guidance

There are two inward ways by which most people feel they are being led. We will look at them one at a time. The first is through their feelings—whether a certain decision leaves them feeling peaceful, or whether it causes emotional turmoil.

Group Discussion: Do you see any problem with this method? What danger might we want to consider in following a certain feeling for guidance?

The problem with this method is the same problem we always have with all our feelings: they fluctuate dramatically and can be very misleading. When making a decision, we must always carefully evaluate them. Is our feeling of peace from God, or is it because the events that are happening are particularly pleasant to us? Is our feeling of unrest because we are out of God's will, or is it because God is leading us to do something rather unpleasant and hard?

Time is probably one of the greatest helps in knowing if our feelings are being influenced by the Spirit of God or even by some endocrine imbalance. If our negative feelings are being caused by our resistance to the known will of God, we need to understand that. And if our positive feelings are only the result of getting our own way, we need to know that, too. As we continue to pray and ask for God's guidance, He will find a way to communicate with us. That is His promise and responsibility.

Personal Desires and Guidance

Another important inward guidance we should consider in making decisions concerning God's will for our lives is that of personal desire.

Group Discussion: How could God use our desires to guide us?

Personal Questions: When are you at your best as far as Christian service is concerned? Does that tell you anything about the part desire plays in finding God's will for your life?

A.W. Tozer says, "Now a happy truth too often overlooked in our anxious search for the will of God is that in the majority of decisions touching our earthly lives, God expresses no choice, but leaves everything to our own preference."

Many of our personal desires were given to us by God.

Read Psalm 10:17.

20. What, according to this verse, does the Lord hear?____________________

21. What is His response? ____________________

Personal Questions: Have you ever wanted something so badly that you ached for it? Did you feel that no one could understand that ache? What did you do about your desire?

Read Psalm 38:9-11.

22. When we are longing for something, what things can the Lord see?____________________

God knows all about us, He knows what our desires are, and if they are good desires, He wants to work within those desires.

The Lord is [rigidly] righteous in all His ways, and gracious and merciful in all His works. The Lord is near to all who call upon Him, to all who call upon Him sincerely and in truth. He will fulfill the desire of those who reverently and worshipfully fear Him, He also will hear their cry, and will save them (Ps. 145:17-19 TAB).

We need to stay before the Lord in prayer, continually humbling ourselves, and calling on Him in sincerity and truth.

Read Mark 11:24 in the King James Version.

23. What will be granted to us when we pray? ______________________________

24. What are the qualifications for that result? ______________________________

Personal Question: Have your desires ever been changed when you sought the Lord in humility, sincerity and truth—when you recognized His righteousness? If you feel comfortable doing so, share it with the others.

Read Psalm 37:4,5.

Here is the bottom line on using desire as a guideline for finding God's will for your life. It begins in the attitude of our heart toward God.

25. What is the qualifications for having the desire of our heart met by God? ______________

____

26. What two further steps are given in verse 5? ______________________________

____

Frequently, we can make a major decision for our life based on the personal desire we have about the matter. If the decision we are making is a life's occupation, we will be happier and have the ability to stay with the occupation longer if it is something we have a *desire* to do. Later, when we are faced with the inevitable sacrifices that come along with such a choice, we will be better able to make those sacrifices.

Personal Question: Write out a dream, goal or desire that you have in your heart.

____

____

____

____

____

____

Personal Questions: Do you think God might allow you to pursue your dream, or that He might grant you that desire? What do you think following your dream might cost you? Are you willing to pay that cost? Paul had much to say on this subject to the Philippians.

Therefore, my dear ones, as you have always obeyed [my suggestions], so now, not only [with the enthusiasm you would show] in my presence but much more because I am absent, work out—cultivate, carry out to the goal and fully complete—your own salvation with reverence and awe and trembling [self-distrust, that is, with serious caution, tenderness of conscience, watchfulness against temptation; timidly shrinking from whatever might offend God and discredit the name of Christ.]

[Not in your own strength] for it is God Who is all the while effectually at work in you—energizing and creating in you the power and desire—both to will and to work for His good pleasure and satisfaction and delight (Phil. 2:12,13 TAB).

God is energizing you, giving you creative desires so that you will be ready to do His will.

Continue at Home

To search yourself

1. What do you desire? Does it involve helping other people? Will it bring personal growth?
2. Could you, on a short term commitment, experiment to find out if your present desires are something you would like to invest the rest of your life in? (Marriage is a lifetime commitment and is not open for experimentation. You need to seek the mind of Christ in the matter of a marriage partner before making that kind of commitment.)
3. Are you willing to put your desires to the test of time?

To do

After you have searched yourself and answered the above questions, write on the following page the things you desire which you believe God may also be leading you to do. Write out some steps, goals, or procedures toward accomplishing those desires.

To memorize

"In all your ways acknowledge him, and he will make your paths straight. Do not be wise in your own eyes; fear the Lord and shun evil" (Prov. 3:6,7).

Keeping Track

The thing I desire which I believe God may be leading me to do	The way it involves helping others	The way it can bring personal growth	A way I experiment to see if I want to spend my life doing this	My test of time

8

Abilities and Obedience

Getting Acquainted: What desire of your heart has the Lord granted you this week? Has God used a desire He has given you, this week or previously, to lead you in a new way? Tell the others about it.

Group Discussion: Read Jeremiah 1:4-10. Have you ever felt like Jeremiah did in this passage? Tell about it. What did you do about it?

The Lesson

God Leads through Abilities and Gifts

Jeannie thinks nothing of planning a dinner for 80 people, but don't ask her to teach a class. It's the easiest thing in the world for her to bake all the pies for a large pie social at her church, but don't ask her to say anything in public.

Sue, on the other hand, has no idea how to begin to plan a big dinner party. She has no idea how much food is needed, how much help to recruit, or even what needs to be done first, second, etc. But she is an effective Bible teacher and is not afraid to speak to large groups.

Why are these two women so different? They are different because God has endowed each woman with special gifts and abilities. Probably, each has found God's plan or *will* for her life and has found her particular place of ministry.

Read 1 Corinthians 12:4-11.

1. What three varieties of things are listed here? ______________________________

2. Who is the Giver of these gifts? ______________________

3. To whom are the gifts, services and works given? ______________________

____

4. List the kinds of gifts which are given.

a. ______________________

b. ______________________

c. ______________________

d. ______________________

e. ______________________

f. ______________________

g. ______________________

h. ______________________

i. ______________________

These are the spiritual gifts that are given to individual Christians. They are not given for our personal pleasure, but for the upbuilding of the church.

Believers may possess more than one of these gifts. In fact, often certain gifts work together.

Read 1 Corinthians 12:28,29.

5. In addition to the spiritual gifts listed above, what other gifts has God given to the Church?

a. ______________________

b. ______________________

c. ______________________

d. ______________________

e. ______________________

f. ______________________

g. ______________________

h. ______________________

These gifts are ministry gifts and are resident in individual believers in the church. Once again, a person may have more than one of these gifts working in her life.

Personal Question: Have you ever taken time to assess the gifts that are resident in your life? Write down in the space provided all of the things you are good at doing. These can be things such as writing letters, arranging flowers, painting houses, or ministering a spiritual gift.

Group Discussion: Think about the leaders in your church. What gifts do you see in operation in their lives that are a blessing to the Church? Do you see any relationship between their gifts and the fact that God has chosen them to lead the church?

God uses our abilities to guide us. A monotone is never going to be called to be an opera star, unless God does a healing of his vocal chords or his ability to distinguish tone, or whatever it is that would be needed to have such a miracle take place. God is going to call someone with a voice to a ministry of music. God will give the monotone some other calling suitable to his abilities.

Look at your list of abilities above. Is there something written there that you have never before thought of offering to God for His use? Write out below the way in which you think God might use that ability.

Even though you have written out your idea of how God might use your ability, you may be surprised at the way in which He will *actually* use it.

There is a story told about a woman whose ability was giving fancy dinner parties. She loved planning the table decorations, the food, the guest list, the seating arrangement. However, she saw no way in which God could use this ability.

One day she talked with her pastor about this ability. For a moment he wasn't sure either how this gift could be used. Then he thought of an idea. "Why don't you plan a dinner at midday each week just for our staff here at the church. It will be a good time of relaxation and fellowship."

So that is what she began to do. She spent many hours planning, preparing, cooking and serving the meal. And what a meal it was! The staff had a wonderful time together, so wonderful in fact that they asked if family members could join them the following week for the meal. Then after a time they began to invite friends. After a period of time the event grew to include more than a hundred people, many of whom were unsaved.

So it was decided that a short, inspirational message would be given and an opportunity to accept Jesus Christ as Lord. That simple luncheon became an evangelistic tool for that church, and many people came to know Christ because of it.

Here was a woman who simply took the talents she had and gave them to God. He, in turn, blessed them and gave them back one-hundred fold.

Bob Pierce, founder of World Vision, once said to a group of students, "The greatest ability anyone can have is availability." God wants us to take whatever He has placed in our hand and give it back to Him so that He can make something beautiful out of it.

Sometimes the way we find out about our abilities is to accept a new responsibility, perhaps even one that seems too hard for us. As we accept that responsibility and begin to walk in faith pursuing it, we grow and grow and grow.

Personal Questions: What has God asked you to do that you think is too hard for you? What is your reaction to the thing He has asked you to do? Do you think, knowing God may be using this thing to guide you, that you could be willing to do what He asks?

Read 1 Peter 4:10.

6. For what purpose are special gifts given? ____________________

Personal Question: How are you using your special gifts?

God Guides through Obedience

Closely tied to the whole subject of guidance is that of obedience. In fact, obedience may be the bottom line in the matter of finding God's will.

Jim Elliott, martyred missionary to Ecuador, once wrote his wife-to-be, "Remember that if we are the sheep of His pasture, we are destined for an altar."

That may not be the happiest idea in the world, but it is more true than we know. For a committed Christian, following God is a life of continual obedience and sacrifice. Take a look at some of the people in the Bible who set out to obey God's will and what it cost them.

Read 1 Samuel 23:15-17.

7. What did Jonathan reaffirm to David here? ______________________

____

David had the anointing of God on his life. He had been chosen to be king of Israel. He certainly knew God's will for his life and yet for a time he was chased all over the kingdom by a mad king. It cost David to do God's will.

Read Exodus 15:22-24.

8. Moses set out to obey God's will by leading the children of Israel into the wilderness and on toward the Promised Land. What happened when he reached the first stop at Marah? ______________________

____

Moses was clearly called of God to lead the people out of Egypt, but many times on their journey to Israel he encountered difficulty, was challenged by the people, and suffered great hardship at the hands of people. It cost Moses to do the will of God.

Read Mark 4:35-38.

9. What happened to the disciples when they did the will of Jesus? ______________________

____

10. What question did they ask Jesus when they awakened Him? ______________________

____

Read Acts 9:26-30.

11. When Paul was converted, he began to preach Christ. What was the reaction among the Christians? ______________________

12. What was the reaction of the Grecian Jews? ______________________

Paul answered the call of God. He knew he was doing the will of God and yet he had to flee for his life. It cost Paul to do the will of God.

Often when we set out to obey the Lord, the next step is testing. At some point most of us will ask ourselves if what we have set out to do is worth it. We may consider returning to a less stressful time in our life. But discipleship, following the will of God, begins with denying self, taking up our cross and following Him.

Group Discussion: Have you ever set out to follow the Lord and immediately had everything start to go wrong? Tell the others about it. Did you give up or go on?

Personal Questions: Now that we have studied the whole subject of guidance from God, would your reaction to a new leading from God be different than previously? How?

____

____

____

____

When you were a baby, you yelled for everything you wanted, and you got it—food, a change of diaper, being held, warmth. Then you began to get a little older and suddenly, instead of coming to hold you a little, your mother decided to let you cry yourself to sleep one night. Like it or not, you grew up a little.

Then one day you reached out to touch some treasured object and Mother said, "No." You cried and began to realize that you couldn't have everything you wanted. Over the years the process was repeated with other things you wanted, which your parents wouldn't let you have, until, hopefully, one day you came to a stage where you had the maturity and strength to deny *yourself.*

Maturity, in part, means the ability to deny oneself. Now no one should have to say, "Don't eat cookies before dinner, you'll spoil your appetite." Your experience and knowledge tell you it is not best for your body that you indulge in sweets just before a meal, because doing so dulls your appetite for the good food it needs.

God does not force us to obey Him. He has given us the gift of freedom—freedom to choose to do His will. When we grow up in Christ, we begin willingly to choose His path. We begin to realize the time has come to deny ourselves and walk with Christ, even if the road leads to a cross.

J.B. Phillips says that to "deny yourself" means "give up all right to yourself."

13. Jesus called to a number of people while He was on earth. Let's look at some of their responses to His call. Write the answers in the blanks below.

	Who was called	Response
Matthew 4:18-22	________________	________________________________
		________________________________
Matthew 9:9	________________	________________________________
		________________________________
Matthew 19:16-22	________________	________________________________
		________________________________

Read Luke 9:23,24.

14. What are the conditions Jesus laid down for following Him?

a. ____

b. ____

c. ____

Sometimes we are willing to deny ourselves, take up our cross daily, and follow Him until we see where that cross is taking us and what it is going to cost us. The rich young man decided that if it were going to cost him everything he had, he didn't really want to go down that road.

Yet no one achieves anything significant without the laying down of his life. No athlete, dancer, singer, or scientist ever made a great contribution to mankind without personal sacrifice.

Listen to the stories of gold-winning Olympic stars. None of them got to be top winners without hours, days, weeks and years of personal sacrifice and self-discipline.

When after we have prayed, the Lord gives us a glimpse of some dark, back alley, we have to decide if we really want to do God's will.

We must always remember, too, that the dark alley may only be a passageway to a large, full, abundant ministry and life with Jesus. Doing God's will, ultimately should bring us to a place of contentment, joy and fulfillment.

Read Jeremiah 29:11-13.

15. What are God's plans regarding us? ______________________________

16. What are the conditions given here? ______________________________

____

This is the secret of finding God's will for our life: To seek Him with all our heart, call upon Him, obey His will, follow hard after Him. Then we *will* find His will.

Continue at home

To search yourself

How is your obedience level? Are you having trouble following God's leading? Obedience begins in the little things of life.

To do

1. On the following page make a list of areas of your life where it is hard for you to obey either another person or the Lord.
2. Decide what you will do to change in this area.
3. Make this decision a matter of daily prayer, of laying down your life and taking up your cross to follow Jesus.
4. Remember that when we learn obedience in little things, He will trust us with greater responsibilities.
5. Expect to grow in your spiritual life as you learn closer obedience to God's will.

To memorize

"Each one should use whatever gift he has received to serve others, faithfully administering God's grace in its various forms" (1 Pet. 4:10).

"Whoever does God's will is my brother and sister and mother" (Mark 3:35).

Keeping Track

I find it hard to obey God in this area: ______________________________

____

____

____

____

____

____

I plan to change this by ______________________________

____

____

____

____

____

____

I find it hard to obey others in this area: ______________________________

____

____

____

____

____

____

I plan to change this by ______________________________

____

____

____

9

Would You Be Willing?

Getting Acquainted: Share with others in the group the ways in which God has specifically guided you this week.

Group Discussion: Tell about a time when God was definitely leading you to do something you were unwilling to do. What happened?

The Lesson

Evaluating Our Willingness

We have seen in our first two lessons that God is a God of love who cares that we find His will. He cares so much that He sometimes intervenes in even miraculous ways, such as in the case of Saul of Tarsus, who became Paul the Apostle. God has promised to guide and is faithful to do so, even when we have trouble hearing His voice.

We need to learn to wait, to listen to His voice, and to be perfectly honest with Him if we do not understand what He is saying to us. We need to ask Him to communicate with us in a way we can understand.

But then comes the next step. God has told us what He wants, but are we willing to follow His leading? Let's take a little test to evaluate what our response might be.

Low---High

Where am I in my desire to know God's will?

1	2	3	4	5	6	7	8

Ability to trust God no matter what happens?

1	2	3	4	5	6	7	8

Willingness to obey God, no matter what He asks?

1	2	3	4	5	6	7	8

Personal Questions: How did you do? Are you surprised at your response? Where if anywhere, were you low?

The Reverend Everett Fullam has said, "There is one citadel God will not storm: my will...there is a throne in my heart. I determine who sits there."

Many of us say, "Yes, I am willing to do what God wants," but when it comes right down to it, we are unwilling. God speaks to us and tries to get us to do His will, but because He has given us the power of choice, He does not force us to do what He wants. Remember Jonah.

Read Jonah 1:1-3.

1. How did the Lord speak to Jonah? ______________________

2. What was he told to do? ______________________

3. Where did he go? ______________________

Read Jonah 2:1,10—3:2.

4. What uncommon circumstances did God use to get Jonah to Nineveh?

____

____

____

5. What command did God give the fish? ______________________

6. When God spoke the second time to Jonah, what did He say?

____

____

____

7. What was Jonah's response this time? ______________________

When Jonah was disobedient, God did not drive him to Nineveh with a whip. Rather, He made his circumstances so uncomfortable that Jonah changed his mind.

The problem is never with God's willingness or ability to guide us, but it is within us. The next problem then is *how to become willing to do God's will.*

Read Luke 18:18-24.

8. What guidance was the ruler asking of Jesus? ______

9. When Jesus told him those things that must be done, what was his reaction? ______

This young man heard from the very lips of Jesus what God's will for his life was, yet he went away and ignored what Jesus told him. He knew the exact will of God and was unwilling to do it.

Personal Question: Perhaps there is something in your life that God is leading you to do and you are unwilling. Can you determine why you are unwilling?

Read Matthew 6:33.

10. What is to be our highest priority in determining God's will? ______

______

11. What will be the end result of seeking his righteousness and kingdom? ______

______

The Amplified Bible says it this way: *"But seek for (aim at and strive after) first of all His kingdom, and His righteousness (His way of doing and being right), and then all these things taken together will be given you besides."*

We are so prone to get it the other way around. We seek for the things we need and want, and fail to seek God's righteousness and His will first. But God has made it very plain in this verse which way it should be. When we walk in His will, other things fall in place.

Personal Question: What problems do you have, or see others having, in following this formula? ______

______

______

Becoming Willing through Knowing God.

Elizabeth Elliott says, "We talk a lot nowadays about people 'doing their own thing.' It is not a very Christian idea when you come right down to it. We were created to do Somebody else's thing—namely, to glorify God and enjoy Him forever."

M. Blaine Smith in *Knowing God's Will** says, "The most important thing I can say is, 'If I am willing to do God's will, I will do it.'"

Group Discussion: How do we become willing? What is the key, the secret?

The key to willingness is our relationship to God. As we come to know Him better, to trust Him more, we will become better able to do His bidding. The more we love Him, the more we will want to please Him, and we will align ourselves with His perfect will.

Read Psalm 135:5,6.

12. What do we learn about God in these verses? ______

The Bible is full of verses like these which give us insights into the personality and characteristics of God. We should daily search for them. As we learn to know more about God, we learn to better trust Him, and our relationship with Him will be enhanced.

**Knowing God's Will*, IVP, Downers Grove, IL 60515, 1979.

Group Discussion: What are some steps you followed in developing a relationship with a person you now love very much?

Our relationship with the Lord could in many respects be compared with developing a relationship with a good friend. At first we meet her and begin to get acquainted. For a time we share on a superficial level, but the better we come to know her, the more we want to please her. We learn to avoid what displeases her and what pleases her. Sometimes we cannot even put our finger on how we know these things; we just know.

So it is with our Lord. The more time we spend in His presence, getting to know Him, learning to love Him, obeying His commands, the more we know what pleases Him. We don't even have to ask. We know! We need to be growing into that kind of relationship with Christ.

Personal Questions: How do you feel when you have shared deeply with a friend who understands you? How do you feel when you know what it is the Lord wants you to do and you have done it?

Becoming Willing through Trust

Group Discussion: Two little girls were standing on a large rock and both wanted to climb down but were afraid to try. Standing below was the father of just one of the girls. "Jump," he said to the first child, "I'll catch you." But she wouldn't jump. No amount of persuasion could convince her it was safe to jump. Finally, he turned to the other little girl and said, "You jump." At that, the second child leaped into the air and into his arms. Which of the two girls was his own child? How do you know? What made the difference?

Confidence, trust, makes the difference for us, too, in the matter of following God's will. When we know our heavenly Father, we will have no hesitation about leaping off into space to do His will. We know He will be there to catch us before we hit bottom. In fact, it can be a lot of fun to leap off into space, if we are sure there is someone there to catch us before we hit bottom. It's risky, but it's exciting!

Read Ruth 2:3 in the New American Standard Bible.

Ruth reveals herself as a woman of faith and trust. She set out to provide for her mother-in-law and her own physical needs by gleaning in a field.

13. What word in verse 3, tells us that God was supernaturally guiding Ruth as she gleaned? ________

____

Personal Question: We quote this familiar passage again and again to remind ourselves that we can trust God. List some of the "all things" of your life in which you need to know God is at work.

We trust God because we've come to know Him. And because we know Him, we do not have to be afraid of failure. We come to understand that we are loved totally just the way we are. We can stop being afraid of failure because God loves us. It makes walking in His will so much easier.

Henri J.M. Nouwen says, "What finally matters is that our hearts become like quiet cells where God can dwell, wherever we go and whatever we do. The more we train ourselves to spend time with God and Him alone, the more we will discover that God is with us at all times and in all places. Then we will be able to recognize Him even in the midst of a busy and active life."

If you want to know what God wants, know God.

Personal Question: There are some steps we can take in coming to know God better. Write out in the space provided a statement about whether you are or are not doing each step and what changes you should make.

Step 1: Have you given God, not just your heart for salvation, but your entire life for His use?

Step 2: Do you believe that God loves you and is concerned that you find His will?

Step 3: Do you read His word and meditate on it, letting it become part of your life?

Step 4: Are you praying and asking God to lead you?

Group Discussion: There is a real tendency, when we are out of fellowship with God, to pull away from Him, to spend less time in His presence, to hold back from Him. What advice would you give to someone who came and confessed that her relationship with God is not good?

Read Psalm 51.

14. David, at the time of writing this psalm, was far from God because of sin in his life. What does this psalm tell us he did about his relationship to God? ______________________

Group Discussion: What can we learn from David about a broken relationship with God?

Personal Questions: Is there anything in your life that has broken your relationship with God? Are you running *from* God with your sin, or *to* Him for forgiveness? In the space below write a prayer expressing how you feel about God and about your spiritual status with Him. Ask for forgiveness and a restoration of your relationship with Him. If this is hard for you, select portions of David's prayer that we have just read and write them out as your prayer.

Always remember that God is willing to work with us. We are His children and He loves us. He thinks we are worth the effort. He will not abandon us to our sin. His Holy Spirit continually strives with us and attempts to pull us back onto the right path.

As we strengthen our relationship with God, other relationships fall into line. We need not even worry about them. We need to continue to use every opportunity to draw closer to God.

Becoming Willing through Fasting

When we are talking about the will of God, most of us have to admit we have a pretty good idea already what God's will is for us. The problem is not usually that we don't know the will of God, but that we aren't willing to do that will. One of the ways to become willing is through fasting.

Read Isaiah 58:1,2.

15. What, upon casual observation, would you say is the spiritual attitude of the people Isaiah addresses? ______

Read Isaiah 58:3.

16. What is the key question they ask in this verse? ______

These people were fasting and going through a spiritual ritual, but God was not listening to them because they were not doing the known will of God. They had been instructed over and over by Isaiah and other prophets about the will of God, and yet they chose to go their own way and do their own thing—practicing idolatry all over the land.

Read Isaiah 58:6-9.

God describes in a very specific way what He wants them to do. He wants them to care for the sick, loosen the chains of injustice, set the oppressed free, etc.

17. When they do the known will of God, then what will happen? ____________________________

____

____

18. In verse 9 there is a great promise that when they have fasted and brought their minds into alignment with the known will of God, God will do something. What is it? ____________________

____

When we fast, it helps to bring our minds into alignment with what we already know to be the will of God. It helps us to concentrate on what God is saying to us, to hear His voice more clearly.

Group Discussion: Can you tell a time when you fasted and God's will was plain to you?

Becoming Willing through Prayer

It is important to pray for God's guidance, and the amount of time spent in prayer should be in proportion to the importance of the decision we are about to make. Important, life-changing decisions demand much prayer. Choices about a life's mate, vocation, life-style, and where to live are important decisions which will affect the rest of your life. These are worth a great deal of prayer.

Prayer is, first of all, an attitude of openness toward God, of listening rather than talking. It is having a heart that says, "What is it, Lord?"

It is having the attitude of Samuel in the Old Testament when he said, *"Speak for your servant is listening" (1 Sam. 3:10).*

Read Daniel 6:8-10.

19. Even though Daniel knew that a document had been signed that said no one was to pray to anyone other than the king, he went ahead and prayed to God. What was his reason for doing so? ____

Daniel was a man of prayer, and no decree from a king was going to stop him from his daily time with the Lord.

Read Daniel 6:16.

20. Where did his faithfulness in devotional prayer lead Daniel? ____________________

Daniel believed it was God's will for him to communicate with Him daily. Doing God's will cost Daniel something. Doing God's will may not always be easy.

Continue at Home

To search yourself

1. Am I willing to do God's will?
2. If I am willing, what do I see as a priority in God's will?

To do

1. Take a concordance and look up the word *know* as it relates to knowing God. As you read, make a list on the following page of the attributes of God you discover. Knowing more about God will help strengthen your relationship with Him.
2. Referring back to the list you made in Chapter eight, in which decision might you now be willing to follow God?
3. If you are unwilling, what do you plan to do about it?
4. Complete the following statement: "I believe becoming willing to do God's will, might lead me to...

To memorize

"But seek first his kingdom and his righteousness, and all these things will be given to you as well. Therefore do not worry about tomorrow for tomorrow will worry about itself. Each day has enough trouble of its own" (Matt. 6:33,34).

Keeping Track

Scripture reference for the word *know* as it relates to knowing God	These are the attributes of God I discovered